Out and About at the Aquarium

By Amy Rechner
Illustrated by Becky Shipe

Special thanks to our advisers for their expertise:

Samantha Norton, Coordinator of School Programs
John G. Shedd Aquarium, Chicago, Ill.

Susan Kesselring, M.A., Literacy Educator
Rosemount-Apple Valley-Eagan (Minnesota) School District

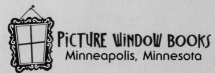

PICTURE WINDOW BOOKS
Minneapolis, Minnesota

The author wishes to thank:

• Samantha Norton, Coordinator of School Programs
  at the John G. Shedd Aquarium in Chicago;

• John Rechner.

Managing Editor: Bob Temple
Creative Director: Terri Foley
Editor: Peggy Henrikson
Editorial Adviser: Andrea Cascardi
Copy Editor: Laurie Kahn
Designer: John Moldstad
Page production: Picture Window Books
The illustrations in this book were prepared digitally.

Picture Window Books
5115 Excelsior Boulevard
Suite 232
Minneapolis, MN 55416
1-877-845-8392
www.picturewindowbooks.com

Library of Congress Cataloging-in-Publication Data
Rechner, Amy.
Out and about at the aquarium / by Amy Rechner ; illustrated by Becky Shipe.
p. cm. — (Field trips)
Includes bibliographical references and index.
Summary: Aquarium worker Ming gives a guided tour of the Blue Harbor
Aquarium, where she explains such things as what kinds of jobs people have
there, what kinds of fish and animals live there, and how food is prepared
for aquarium dwellers. Includes an activity and other learning resources.
ISBN 1-4048-0298-3 (reinforced lib. bdg.)
1. Aquariums, Public—Juvenile literature. 2. Aquatic animals—Juvenile
literature. [1. Aquariums, Public. 2. Aquatic animals.] I. Shipe, Becky, ill.
II. Title. III. Field trips (Picture Window Books)
QL78 .R43 2004
597.073—dc22
                                        2003016155

We're going on a field trip to the aquarium.
We can't wait!

Things to find out:

Does an aquarium just have fish?

How do they take care of the animals
at the aquarium?

Can we touch any of the animals?

Do the big fish ever eat the little fish?

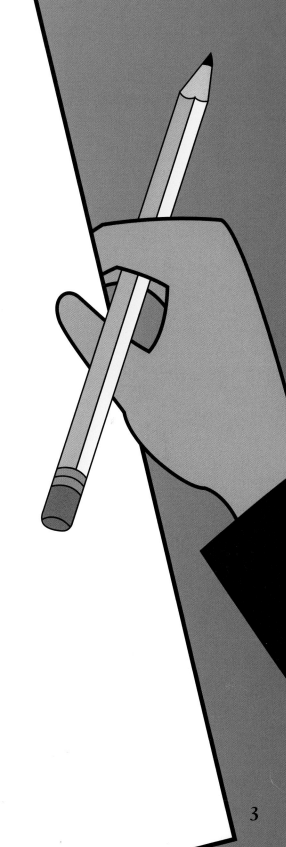

Welcome to Blue Harbor Aquarium! My name is Ming. We have more than 900 different kinds of animals living here—not just fish. All of our animals need to live next to or in the water. The aquarium provides places for the animals to live that are similar to their natural homes in the wild. The area where an animal lives is called its habitat. Our aquarium has both ocean habitats and freshwater habitats, which are like ponds, lakes, or wetlands.

Besides fish, an aquarium houses:

- birds (such as penguins);
- mammals (such as whales and dolphins);
- amphibians (such as frogs);
- reptiles (such as turtles);
- crustaceans (such as lobsters and crabs);
- mollusks (such as clams and oysters);
- sea plants (such as kelp).

5

Our first stop is the coral reef. A coral reef can look like a big pile of colorful plants or rocks under the sea. But a reef is actually made of the skeletons of many tiny animals called coral. Some of these animals are still living. Coral grows in tropical oceans in warm or hot areas of the world. A coral reef provides food and homes for other creatures that live in and around it.

There's one of our scuba divers. His job is to get a close look at the animals to make sure they're healthy. Imagine swimming with sharks every day! The scuba diver may also feed the animals or clean the inside of the glass.

A fish specialist who works in an aquarium is called an aquarist. Aquarists don't always need to go in the water. People who work with animals other than fish also work in aquariums.

7

Here's our touch pool, where you can actually feel a starfish.

We bring in animals from all around the world. We want everyone to know about these interesting creatures so people will help take care of them.

This aquarium holds fish from the oceans around
Asia, Africa, and Australia.

The protection of animals and nature is called conservation. Without conservation, rare plants and animals might disappear forever. One way you can help is by not littering. When trash gets into any natural habitat, an animal might eat it by mistake and get sick or die.

Our next stop is the oceanarium, where the dolphins, whales, and penguins live.
We train the dolphins to follow commands. This helps us to take care of them.
For example, we taught the dolphins to open their mouths wide so we can
check their teeth. The dolphin show is our way of practicing commands.
It's fun to watch, too!

Dolphins and whales make lots of different noises. We have microphones in the habitats so you can hear them. Dolphins make squeaks, chirps, and clicks. Whales make low, humming sounds.

An oceanarium is a large saltwater aquarium that has both indoor and outdoor habitats. It has different viewing levels, so visitors can watch the animals moving both above and under the water.

There are many different kinds of whales. We have two kinds here at Blue Harbor. One is the black-and-white orca. The other kind is the beluga whale. Beluga whales are smaller than orcas, but they're still very, very big. They weigh about as much as two classrooms of children put together!

Whales live in cold water. A thick layer of fat, called blubber, keeps them warm. The blubber helps them float, too.

Dolphins and whales aren't fish. They are mammals, which means they nurse their babies. Cats, dogs, and people are other kinds of mammals.

13

Look at the sea otters! They live in cold water. But they don't have a layer of fat or blubber to keep them warm like whales, dolphins, and seals do. Instead, sea otters have thick fur that traps tiny air bubbles to keep them warm.

14

An otter's coat has about a million hairs in 1 square inch (6½ square centimeters). This is more hairs than grow on a whole human head. Otters spend a lot of time rolling around, combing themselves, and blowing air into their fur to trap more air bubbles.

15

The penguins live in their own habitat. It's very cold in there! They have their own sunrise and sunset, which we create with lights. We make it get light and dark according to the times of sunrise and sunset in the penguins' natural habitat.

The air temperature in the penguin habitat is 38 degrees Fahrenheit (3 degrees Celsius). The water temperature is only 48 degrees Fahrenheit (9 degrees Celsius). These temperatures are not much above freezing, which is 32 degrees Fahrenheit (0 degrees Celsius).

This is the kitchen, where we prepare the food. It's a lot of work to feed all these animals! We feed them several times a day, so they don't need to hunt for their food. This means they don't eat each other, as they would in the wild.

Now you've seen many kinds of animals and how we care for them at the aquarium. I hope you enjoyed your visit to Blue Harbor. There's a lot to see and learn here, so please come back soon!

MAKE YOUR OWN AQUATIC ANIMALS

You don't need to worry about feeding these salt-dough aquatic animals. Just enjoy them!

What you need:

2 cups flour
1 cup salt
1 medium-sized bowl
a large spoon
cold water
small bowls—1 for each color you want
food coloring in several colors

What you do:

1. Pour the flour and salt into the bowl, and mix them with the spoon.

2. Add small amounts of water, and stir until the mixture is easy to shape, like soft clay.

3. Divide the dough into separate bowls for each color you want, leaving some dough in the first mixing bowl so you have some you can use for white.

4. Mix a few drops of food coloring into the dough in each bowl. You may want several colors to make rainbow fish. If you want to make a penguin, make sure you have black. (And that white you saved will come in handy, too.)

5. Use the dough to make aquatic animals, such as bright-colored tropical fish, an octopus, a shark, an orca whale, a crab, and a penguin.

6. Let the dough animals harden overnight.

7. Sort your animals according to whether they are warm-water animals or cold-water animals. Then sort them according to where they live in the ocean. Do they crawl on the bottom of the ocean, swim in the middle, or play near the top? Are they fish or mammals?

FUN FACTS

- Emperor penguins can easily swim 14 miles (24 kilometers) an hour—and can reach 31 miles (50 kilometers) an hour in short bursts. They can dive 1,500 feet (460 meters) below the surface to catch fish. That's as deep as a 150-story building is high! These penguins can stay underwater for 20 minutes or more.

- A beluga whale is about as big as a car. Adult belugas range from 12 to 16 feet (3½ to 5 meters) long and weigh from 1,100 to 3,300 pounds (500 to 1,500 kilograms). When a beluga can get it, the whale will eat at least 50 to 60 pounds (23 to 26 kilograms) of food a day.

- Blue whales are five to almost six times bigger than beluga whales. In fact, the blue whale is the largest animal on earth. One blue whale can weigh up to 150 tons (136 metric tons). That's 300,000 pounds (136,200 kilograms)—as much as 90 large beluga whales! Aquariums don't house blue whales. Can you imagine feeding them?

- Sea horses are actually a kind of fish. They swim upright. When they want to stay in one place, they curl their tails around sea grasses and hold on tight. The father sea horse gives birth to the babies in a pouch on his belly.

- Sharks were on earth long before dinosaurs. Scientists have found shark fossils that are about 400 million years old. Dinosaurs started roaming the earth only 248 million years ago!

GLOSSARY

amphibian—an animal that lives in the water when it is young and on land as an adult. Some amphibians, such as frogs, can live both in the water and on land as adults.

aquarist—a person who works with fish in an aquarium

aquatic—growing or living in water all or most of the time

blubber—a layer of fat

conservation—the protection of animals and plants, as well as the wise use of what we get from nature

fish—a cold-blooded animal that lives in the water, has scales on its body, a fin or fins for swimming, and gills for breathing underwater

habitat—the place and natural conditions in which a plant or an animal lives. An aquarium habitat includes whatever is usually found in an animal's home environment in the wild. It also is kept at the normal temperature of the animal's natural environment.

mammal—a warm-blooded animal that nurses its young

oceanarium—a large saltwater aquarium with indoor and outdoor habitats

TO LEARN MORE

At the Library

Aliki. *My Visit to the Aquarium.* New York: HarperCollins, 1993.

Esbensen, Barbara Juster. *Baby Whales Drink Milk.* New York: HarperCollins, 1994.

Hodge, Judith. *Penguins.* Hauppauge, N.Y.: Barron's, 1999.

Pratt-Serafini, Kristin Joy. *A Swim Through the Sea.* Nevada City, Calif.: DAWN Publications, 1994.

Rustad, Martha E. H. *Jellyfish.* Mankato, Minn.: Pebble Books, 2003.

On the Web

Fact Hound offers a safe, fun way to find Web sites related to this book. All of the sites on Fact Hound have been researched by our staff.
http://www.facthound.com

1. Visit the Fact Hound home page.
2. Enter a search word related to this book, or type in this special code: 1404802983.
3. Click on the FETCH IT button.

Your trusty Fact Hound will fetch the best sites for you!

INDEX